POSSIBLE WORLDS

by John Mighton

Playwrights Canada Press
Toronto • Canada

Playwrights Canada Press
The Canadian Drama Publisher

215 Spadina Ave., Suite 230, Toronto, Ontario, Canada M5T 2C7
phone 416.703.0013   fax 416.408.3402
orders@playwrightscanada.com • www.playwrightscanada.com

The publisher acknowledges the support of the Canadian taxpayers through the Government of Canada Book Publishing Industry Development Program, the Canada Council for the Arts, the Ontario Arts Council, and the Ontario Media Development Corporation.

Cover painting by John Mighton
Cover design by JLArt

Library and Archives Canada Cataloguing in Publication

Mighton, John, 1957-
Possible worlds
2nd rev. ed.
A play
First edition published under title: Possible worlds and A short history of night

ISBN 978-0-88754-562-7

PS8576.I29P68 1997   C812'.54   C97-932516-1
PR9199.3.M53P68 1997

Sixth printing: February 2009
Printed and bound by Hignell Printing, Winnipeg, Manitoba Canada

For Raegan

AUTHOR'S NOTE

I would like to thank Daniel Brooks and Melanie Joseph for the significant dramaturgical work they did on the script, and Michael Devine and Don Kugler for their helpful suggestions.

— *John Mighton*

John Mighton has lectured in Philosophy at McMaster University and is currently completing a Ph.D. in Mathematics at the University of Toronto. His plays, which include *Scientific Americans*, *A Short History of Night*, *Body and Soul*, and *The Little Years*, have been performed across Canada as well as in Europe and the United States. They have won several national awards, including a Governor General's Literary Award for Drama in 1992, for the Playwrights Canada Press publication of *Possible Worlds & A Short History of Night*.

Possible Worlds was first produced by the Canadian Stage Company, November 1990, at the St. Lawrence Centre, Toronto, with the following cast:

WILLIAMS	*Oliver Dennis*
BERKLEY	*Bruce McFee*
GEORGE	*Richard Greenblatt*
JOYCE	*Paula Wing*
PENFIELD	*Daniel Brooks*

Directed by Peter Hinton
Produced by Gregory Nixon
Assistant directed by Brian Quirt
Stage managed by Tony Ambrosi
Set & lighting design by Stephen Droege
Costumes & props designed by Denyse Karn
Sound design by Allen Cole and Michel Charbonneau

A revised version of *Possible Worlds* was produced in 1997 by the Possible Worlds Company, Platform 9 and Theatre Passe Muraille, in Toronto, with the following cast:

WILLIAMS	*Jonathan Wilson*
BERKLEY	*Jim Warren*
GEORGE	*Randy Hughson*
JOYCE	*Pamela Sinha*
PENFIELD	*Chris Earle*

Directed by Daniel Brooks
Stage managed by Melissa Berney
Lighting design by Andrea Lundy
Lighting Operation by Melissa Berney
Sound design by Richard Feren
Set Design by Michael Levine and Julie Fox
Costume Design by Heather MacCrimmon
Produced by Robin Fulford and Taylor Rath
Production Manager: T.J. Shamata

The Characters

GEORGE, *in his Thirties*

JOYCE, *in her Thirties*

BERKLEY, *a detective*

WILLIAMS, *his assistant*

PENFIELD, *a neurologist*

The doctor, business people, and other small roles can be doubled. The doubling need not be heavily disguised.

The Setting

A bachelor apartment. Various rooms and offices.

Scene One

The lights rise. Downstage: a body covered by a blood stained sheet. A man sits nearby. A second man enters.

BERKLEY   What have you got for me, Williams?

WILLIAMS   Break in, homicide.

BERKLEY   That's the fifth this week. Must be a gang war. They're killing each other off.

WILLIAMS   This one is a little different, chief.

BERKLEY   Why? What'd they get?

WILLIAMS   His brain.

Pause.

BERKLEY   What?

WILLIAMS   That's all they took.

BERKLEY   His brain?

BERKLEY *lifts the sheet.*

BERKLEY   Holy shit... what the....

WILLIAMS   He had a thousand dollars in his pocket.

BERKLEY   (*still looking*) Holy shit....

WILLIAMS	Broker. George Barber. We're running a background check....
BERKLEY	Where's the top of his head?
WILLIAMS	Right here, chief.

> *WILLIAMS produces a plastic bag that holds a piece of skull with some hair on it.*

BERKLEY	What'd they use? A skill saw?
WILLIAMS	There aren't any abrasions.
BERKLEY	Can you get money for a brain?
WILLIAMS	Not that I know of.
BERKLEY	Check all the hospitals... especially the university clinic.
WILLIAMS	Right.
BERKLEY	And get that background check to me as soon as possible.
WILLIAMS	Yes sir. (*turning to leave*) What are you doing?
BERKLEY	Thinking... running over some possibilities.
WILLIAMS	Have fun.

Black.

Scene Two

> *Lights up.* JOYCE *sits reading a paper in a crowded restaurant.* GEORGE *enters with food.*

GEORGE   Do you mind if I sit here?

JOYCE   No, go ahead.

> GEORGE *continues to stand.*

GEORGE   (*with great intensity*) There's no place else.

JOYCE   That's fine.

> GEORGE *sits.* JOYCE *continues to read.*

GEORGE   Did you see the article about the magnetized babies?

JOYCE   No.

GEORGE   What about those missing brains?

JOYCE   What paper was this in?

GEORGE   *The National Enquirer.*

JOYCE   I don't read *The Enquirer.*

GEORGE   I do... sometimes. For a joke... those guys have some imagination.

> *Pause.* JOYCE *continues to read, trying to ignore him.*

GEORGE   I'm George.

JOYCE   Joyce.

GEORGE   I've seen you somewhere before.

JOYCE   I don't think so.

GEORGE   Are you from this city?

JOYCE   I live here, yes.

GEORGE   No, I mean originally.

JOYCE   I grew up in a little northern town. You probably wouldn't have heard of it.

GEORGE   What's it called?

JOYCE   Novar.

GEORGE   Really? I grew up there too.

> *Pause.*

JOYCE   What part of Novar?

GEORGE   East Lake. Right out near the filling station.

JOYCE   You went to school there?

GEORGE   Sure.

JOYCE   What did you say your name was?

GEORGE   George Barber.

JOYCE   It's funny.... I don't remember you.

GEORGE   Well, I looked very different back then.

JOYCE	You must have. There were only a hundred people in the high school.
GEORGE	I remember you. You used to swim in the Regatta. You could hold your breath longer than anyone.

Pause.

GEORGE	D'you work around here?
JOYCE	I teach at the University.
GEORGE	Neurology?
JOYCE	That's right. How did you know?
GEORGE	Just a feeling.
JOYCE	What d'you do? Read minds?
GEORGE	I'm a risk analyst.
JOYCE	What's that? Some kind of broker?
GEORGE	No. I advise companies on the risks of investing in various countries.
JOYCE	You must travel a lot.
GEORGE	I've been everywhere.
JOYCE	Must be quite a change from Novar.
GEORGE	Oh well... you always miss your roots.

Pause.

GEORGE	You're very beautiful.
JOYCE	Oh please.
GEORGE	You should have been a model.

JOYCE	That's the last thing I'd want to do.
GEORGE	D'you ever think you might have done something different?
JOYCE	No....
GEORGE	Why not?
JOYCE	I'm a fatalist. I think it's pretty silly to wish things were different from what they are.
GEORGE	(*interrupting*) But you could....
JOYCE	When people see their lives as being different they always make the most trivial changes: if only I'd gone to that party, or taken that job. They never say: if only I'd had two brains or been able to photosynthesize my food. It's as if they think the smaller variations are more likely to have occurred, that God might have overlooked them, but that's just superstition. How could anything be different from what it is?
GEORGE	But surely you've wished you could do things over.
JOYCE	You only have one life — why waste it dreaming about things that could never have happened?
GEORGE	D'you ever fantasize when you make love?
	Pause.
JOYCE	What?
GEORGE	I mean... surely you must use your... sometimes... when you....
JOYCE	No.
	Pause.
GEORGE	I don't believe in promiscuity.

JOYCE	Neither do I. (*standing*) I've got to get back the lab.
GEORGE	How about a show tomorrow night?
JOYCE	I'm working.
GEORGE	What about the weekend?
JOYCE	I'm going to Novar.

Pause.

GEORGE	Maybe I'll see you here again....
JOYCE	I doubt it.

Black.

Scene Three

> GEORGE *sits in an office. An*
> *INTERVIEWER leafs through some*
> *papers.*

INTERVIEWER   You used to work for Merrill Lynch?

GEORGE   That's right.

INTERVIEWER   Mr. Parfit recommended you highly. He said you were "uncanny."

GEORGE   Mr. Parfit is a nice man.

> *Pause.*

INTERVIEWER   I'm going to read you some questions. It's something we do with all our applicants. Some of them involve some math you may not be familiar with. Don't worry if you can't get them all.

GEORGE   Thank you.

INTERVIEWER   They were developed by a philosopher at Harvard. Eric Goodman. Does that name ring a bell?

GEORGE   No.

INTERVIEWER   He made a fortune teaching ethics to bankers. (*laughs*)   Ah, Goodman. Developed the Goodman Theory of Rational Benevolence.

GEORGE   He sounds like a very interesting man.

INTERVIEWER	Oh, yeah. These questions involve some numbers. You're allowed to use a calculator.
GEORGE	That's alright.

Pause.

INTERVIEWER	You can change your mind if you want.
GEORGE	Thank you.
INTERVIEWER	(*reading*) A pharmaceutical company called Gentech introduces a new treatment for Alzheimer's. Shortly after, it is found to cause irreversible hair loss. The affected patients file a class-action law suit. The value of Gentech falls by over 50%. You're then offered an option to buy 150,000 shares of Gentech at thirty-five dollars a share. If the lawsuit is settled out of court, you stand to make a 60% return. If it goes to trial, you'll lose a million dollars. Now George — You can pay the Vice President of Gentech half a million dollars to tell you if they've settled, but there's only a 78.2% chance he'll tell you the truth if they've settled, and only a 49% chance if they haven't. As far as you know, there's a 63% chance they have settled. Do you pay the Vice President?
GEORGE	No.
INTERVIEWER	Why not?
GEORGE	It's a trick question.
INTERVIEWER	What d'you mean?
GEORGE	Using the numbers you gave me, it's worth buying no matter what he says.

Pause.

INTERVIEWER	You did the sums in your head?

GEORGE   Yes.

                    Pause.

INTERVIEWER   The next question is a little more difficult.
                    (*reading*) You own a pharmaceutical company...
                    D'you want some paper?

GEORGE   No.

                    Pause.

INTERVIEWER   (*reading*) You own a pharmaceutical company.
                    Your staff has just manufactured a new batch of
                    acne pills. Normally they test them by feeding
                    them to a hundred rats and observing how many
                    die. From their previous experience, they have a
                    good idea of how many rats will die if the batch
                    is defective. Unfortunately, due to an irregularity
                    in manufacturing this particular batch....

                    Lights fade.

Scene Four

GEORGE *is drinking in a crowded bar.*
JOYCE *enters carrying a drink.*

JOYCE   Can I sit here?

GEORGE   Sure.

JOYCE   This place has gotten pretty popular.

GEORGE   Yes.

JOYCE   Five years ago, when I first started selling
stocks, nobody would come here. Too seedy.

Pause.

JOYCE   You don't know me but... I saw you coming out
of Carson's office this afternoon. Jumping ship?

GEORGE   Yes.

JOYCE   How'd it go?

GEORGE   Great.

Pause.

JOYCE   I guess you're celebrating.

GEORGE   I guess so.

JOYCE   You don't seem too thrilled.

GEORGE   I'm not.

                 Pause.

JOYCE   I've heard about you. You're very good. Why
                 the change? Money?

GEORGE   No.

JOYCE   Sure.... Give yourself a few years. You'll be just
                 like everybody.

                 GEORGE *laughs.*

JOYCE   What's so funny?

GEORGE   I *am* everybody.

                 Pause.

JOYCE   What's that? Some kind of private joke?

GEORGE   I could have all the money I want.

JOYCE   Couldn't we all.

GEORGE   I know things.

JOYCE   Don't tell me.... I've had enough of that kind of
                 information.

GEORGE   This isn't the type of information they can
                 prosecute you for.

JOYCE   Who's your source?

GEORGE   I am.

                 Pause.

GEORGE   I know everything.

JOYCE   What's my name?

GEORGE   Joyce.

Pause.

JOYCE   That's easy, everyone here knows me. You were staring at me the other night. You spend a lot of time here.

GEORGE   D'you believe in other lives?

JOYCE   Past lives?

GEORGE   No, I mean lives going on right now.

JOYCE   Like being in two places at once?

GEORGE   More than two. A lot more.

JOYCE   You must be a great broker, being in hundreds of places at once.

GEORGE   I'm talking about possible worlds. Each of us exists in an infinite number of possible worlds. In one world I'm talking to you right now but your arm is a little to the left, in another world you're interested in that man over there with the glasses, in another you stood me up two days ago — and that's how I know your name.

Pause.

JOYCE   When did you first realize you were more than one person?

GEORGE   In another life.

JOYCE   Oh?

GEORGE   Seventh grade.

JOYCE   Must have been puberty.

GEORGE   No, it was math.

JOYCE laughs.

GEORGE   I was writing a math test in the seventh grade. I was stuck on the last problem. I could see two ways of doing it, but I wasn't sure which would work. Half way through my calculations I suddenly saw myself doing the problem the other way. Only I wasn't just *seeing* myself. For a moment I was actually doing the problem the other way. I looked at my hand and saw a scar. I remembered how I had gotten it. I remembered the dog that had bitten me. Only I'd never been bitten by a dog.

Pause.

JOYCE   How old are you?

GEORGE   Thirty-four.

JOYCE   How many lovers have you had?

GEORGE   That I can remember?

JOYCE   Yes.

GEORGE   Billions.

Pause.

JOYCE   Let's go.

Black.

Scene Five

*Darkness. Sound of animals in cages.
Lights up on BERKELY and a scientist.
A metal box on the scientist's desk
supports a small glass case. The case is
full of wires and fluid, and contains the
brain of a rat.*

SCIENTIST   Would you like to see the animals?

BERKLEY   Yes.... Thank you.

SCIENTIST   This is a citation I received for my work on
primate nervous systems.

BERKLEY   (*pointing offstage*) What's that?

SCIENTIST   My tank.

BERKLEY   Your tank?

SCIENTIST   My sensory deprivation chamber. I spend a lot of
time in there. Not something my colleagues are
too keen about....

*A light flashes on the rat's box.
BERKLEY approaches and examines it.*

BERKLEY   What's this?

SCIENTIST   The brain of a rat.

BERKLEY   Is it alive?

SCIENTIST   Oh yes.... Right now it thinks it's pressing a lever for some food. That's why the light flashed. Every time it flashes, we send an electrical impulse to make it think it's been rewarded.

Pause.

BERKLEY   D'you mind if I take this in?

SCIENTIST   That's alright. I've got dozens of them.

BERKLEY   Dozens?

SCIENTIST   Some biologists believe that natural processes create a field of information. Everything you think, Inspector, even the most trivial fantasy, leaves a trace, a disturbance in that field. I'm trying to learn how to control those disturbances.

BERKLEY   Are you talking about telepathy?

SCIENTIST   Something like that.

A monkey screeches.

BERKLEY   D'you have any brains of... larger animals?

SCIENTIST   Like humans?... I read the papers, Inspector. You think I'm stealing brains.

BERKLEY   We have to investigate every possibility.

SCIENTIST   We're years away from doing this with human brains. We may never be able to do this. Not that the public understands. They'll probably be picketing this place tomorrow.

BERKLEY   Some people might find your research a little frightening.

SCIENTIST   The question is why do we have imaginations? A rat can only imagine so much. It's limited by the structure of it's brain. (*light flashes*) Creatures like us, that can anticipate possible futures and make contingency plans have an evolutionary advantage. We'd be foolish not to use our imaginations, not to investigate every possible fact.

BERKLEY   What can you use a brain for?

SCIENTIST   Oh, plenty of things. I'm sure you've got some ideas.

BERKLEY   All of the people killed have been very intelligent, in positions of power. I think someone is extracting information from them.

SCIENTIST   Maybe. But there are other possibilities. I think you should consider every possibility.... Even aliens.

BERKLEY   Well if you hear from any let me know.

SCIENTIST   You're leaving?

BERKLEY   Yes.

SCIENTIST   Take care of Louise.

BERKLEY   Louise?

SCIENTIST   She's the most intelligent. Her frontal lobes are perfect.

The rat's food light goes on.

SCIENTIST   She's having a snack.

BERKLEY   I'll be in touch.

Black.

Scene Six

> JOYCE *is reading in a crowded restaurant, as in Scene Two. GEORGE enters. It should seem, at first, as if their first meeting is being repeated.*

GEORGE   D'you mind if I sit here?

JOYCE   No, go ahead.

> GEORGE *continues to stand.*

GEORGE   There's no place else.

JOYCE   That's fine.

> GEORGE *sits.* JOYCE *continues to read.*

GEORGE   Did you see the article about the magnetized babies?

JOYCE   What paper was this.... (*she looks at* GEORGE) Oh.

GEORGE   I haven't seen you here in a while.

JOYCE   I've been eating at the lab.

GEORGE   I hope I'm not bothering you.

JOYCE   No.

> *She continues to read.*

GEORGE	You must be very busy.
JOYCE	(*curtly*) I am.

JOYCE *goes back to her paper.*

GEORGE	What d'you do exactly?
JOYCE	I'm looking for ways to increase intelligence.
GEORGE	Maybe you could help me.
JOYCE	I specialize in rat cortexes.

JOYCE *continues reading.*

GEORGE	It must be very interesting.
JOYCE	It's not just that. There's a lot of unnecessary suffering in the world. No political system has ever given people what they want. But neurology will. One day we'll be able to dial and focus our nervous systems the way we adjust our TVs. There will be drugs to extend our lives, increase our intelligence, drugs to erase unpleasant memories. People will look back on the present age with pity. We'll seem like animals to them.

Pause.

GEORGE	How's the dessert?

JOYCE *laughs.*

GEORGE	What?
JOYCE	A few years ago my life was very complicated. There wasn't a day when I could just relax and forget my responsibilities. So I decided I would try to simplify things. At the cafeteria they served three kinds of dessert: chocolate pudding, a kind of sponge cake, and fruit salad. I decided one

day that whenever I was at the counter I wouldn't think. I would always take the fruit salad. I've kept it up ever since — five years.

GEORGE   Don't you think that's a little fanatical?

JOYCE   Probably.

GEORGE   D'you make a lot of resolutions?

JOYCE   All the time.

GEORGE   I remember you at school — always carrying books.

JOYCE   I read all the time. In every book there was always one thing I didn't understand. That would lead me to the next book. I read through whole libraries searching for the secret.

GEORGE *laughs.*

JOYCE   You don't say much about yourself.

GEORGE   There's not much to tell. My wife used to say....

JOYCE   Your wife?

GEORGE   She died several years ago.... An accident.

JOYCE   I'm sorry.

Pause.

GEORGE   It was after she died that I started to travel.

JOYCE   You must have had a very interesting life.

GEORGE   Not really.... I usually find myself in a deck chair by the water. I love summer evenings by the water. I like it at dusk, when the water has that grey tint that seems to contain every other colour.

Pause.

JOYCE	It figures.
GEORGE	What?
JOYCE	That you'd like grey.
GEORGE	I suppose you like black and white.
JOYCE	I've always thought there should be a single clear answer to every question.
GEORGE	Even in love?
JOYCE	Especially in love. I don't trust people who fall in love over and over. They're usually the worst liars.
GEORGE	You're right. I've never understood people who say, "I used to be in love with that person." I don't think you ever stop loving. If you do, you weren't in love in the first place.

> JOYCE *looks at her watch and puts some change on the table.*

JOYCE	I've got to get back to the lab.
GEORGE	How about dinner Thursday?
JOYCE	I've got to work late.
GEORGE	If you weren't so busy, would you go out with me?
JOYCE	If I wasn't so busy I'd be a different person.

> JOYCE *turns to go.*

GEORGE	Listen, give me a chance. I've never met anyone like you, and I've met alot of people.

> JOYCE *hands him her card.*

JOYCE	Call me.

Scene Seven

> WILLIAMS *sits reading the paper.*
> BERKLEY *enters carrying the apparatus*
> *containing the rat's brain.*

WILLIAMS   Morning, chief.

BERKLEY   Morning.

> BERKLEY *puts the box on his desk.*

WILLIAMS   I checked out the first guy — George Barber?
Apparently he and his wife had a big fight
minutes before the murder — over a present
some guy had given her. She walked out on him.

BERKLEY   Alright... good.

> BERKLEY *sits and starts writing.*

WILLIAMS   Did you see this article in the paper?

BERKLEY   No.

WILLIAMS   It says here that black holes were invented to
confuse Russian scientists.... I always thought
there was something fishy about them. What's
that?

BERKLEY   (*ironically*) A present for my wife.

> WILLIAMS *examines the apparatus*
> *closely.*

WILLIAMS   Is it your anniversary?

BERKLEY   My what?

WILLIAMS   Your anniversary?

        BERKLEY *shakes his head in disbelief, continues working.*

WILLIAMS   What does it do?

BERKLEY   Do?

WILLIAMS   Yeah.

BERKLEY   It doesn't do anything.

        The rat's food light goes on.

WILLIAMS   It's some kind of lamp?

BERKLEY   It's not a present. It's the brain of a rat!

WILLIAMS   Oh.

        Pause. WILLIAMS *examines it.*

WILLIAMS   Is it alive?

BERKLEY   She. Her name is Louise.

WILLIAMS   What d'you suppose she's thinking about right now?

        Pause.

WILLIAMS   A normal person thinks about sex every two minutes. You think it's the same with rats?

        Pause.

WILLIAMS   What if we were in a tank like that? We'd never know it.

BERKLEY   Not you.

WILLIAMS   Maybe someone's making us think whatever they want us to. Maybe that's why all those brains are being stolen! Maybe someone's already stolen ours.

BERKLEY   Why would they want your brain Williams?! What d'you normally think about in the course of a day? Your wife? Your house? Hockey? Why would they want to steal your brain and make you think about hockey all the time? What's the motivation?

         Pause.

WILLIAMS   You tell me.

         Pause.

WILLIAMS   Listen, I've been meaning to ask you something.

BERKLEY   What?

WILLIAMS   My wife thinks I should take this course.

BERKLEY   What course?

WILLIAMS   Listen to this. (*reading from a newspaper clipping.*) "The future is here. Join the revolution that does away with dull drills and droning lessons. Increase your creativity and boost your IQ. This course puts you where you belong — on the fast track to superintelligence."

BERKLEY   It couldn't hurt.

WILLIAMS   It has a money-back guarantee.

BERKLEY   Good.

WILLIAMS   I'll phone them now.

BERKLEY   What are you going to do when you're more
                     intelligent, Williams?

WILLIAMS   Solve this case.

Scene Eight

A sonata plays. JOCELYN, *played by* JOYCE, *addresses the audience.*

JOCELYN   Hi. I'm Jocelyn. I'd like to welcome you to the Consciousness Revolution. Over the next few months — if you decide to stay with us beyond this class — I'll be teaching you to use your brains in an entirely new way. You'll learn how to read faster, remember what you learn, create new ideas and coordinate the activity of your right and left hemispheres. Many of you, on graduating, will be able to repeat a thousand phrases from memory after one hearing.

Now at this point some of you may be thinking — that sounds hard. It's been a long day. Perhaps you're saying to yourself — is it worth it? Why should I drag myself here after eight hours of work when I could be at home with someone I love, having a drink, watching TV? For those of you who think that way, I have only one question — Why be dumb when you can be smart?

The theme of tonight's session is Imagination. "Imagination rules the world." Does anyone here know who said that? Napoleon said that. He used to go through all his battles in his mind weeks before he fought them. Tonight we're going to do some exercises for our imaginations. We'll start with a visualization exercise which I'd like you to score. As I ask you to imagine things, and assign yourself points as follows: 3 points if the image is very clear, 2 points — clear, 1 point — unclear, and 0 if you can't imagine anything.

Alright, is everyone ready? You can close your eyes if you want.

See yourself throwing a ball.

Picture the house you grew up in.

Picture a close relative standing in front of you.

Is everyone scoring?

> *Black. The rest of* JOCELYN's *instructions are played on a tape in the darkness.*

JOCELYN Picture the eyes of someone you love.

Feel their hand caressing your face.

See yourself lying in their arms.

Imagine a cold wind when it's raining.

Scene Nine

> GEORGE *sleeping.* JOYCE *shakes him.*

JOYCE Hey, wake up. I'm just making some coffee. I hope you don't have anything important to do today. It's ten.

GEORGE What?

JOYCE I think Kaufman Brothers can survive the morning without me.

GEORGE You work for Kaufman Brothers?

JOYCE What's the matter with you? You weren't *that* drunk last night.

GEORGE What's that smell?

JOYCE Coffee. I said I'm making coffee.

> GEORGE *holds his head.*

JOYCE Is something wrong?

GEORGE My head.

JOYCE You're hung over.

GEORGE No.

JOYCE You want some aspirin?

GEORGE   No, I'm fine. I'm sorry.

                    GEORGE *starts dressing. The phone
                    rings.* JOYCE *watches it.*

GEORGE   Aren't you going to answer it?

JOYCE   No, it's probably my office.

GEORGE   What if they fire you?

JOYCE   I hate my job.

GEORGE   Why?

JOYCE   I've never felt comfortable selling things you
                    can't see or touch.

                    The phone stops.

JOYCE   I guess I'll never know who it was.

GEORGE   What do you sell exactly?

JOYCE   Stocks.

GEORGE   Where were you born?

JOYCE   Right here.

GEORGE   I thought you said Novar....

JOYCE   I think you've got me mixed up with someone
                    else.

                    Pause.

JOYCE   I'm not usually so aggressive in bars. But you
                    looked so lonely sitting there in the middle of all
                    that activity. The whole world could have
                    disappeared and you would have just sat there
                    absorbed in your thoughts. I don't think I've ever

seen anyone that looked so alone in my life....
Except for some married men I know.... You're
not married are you?

GEORGE   My wife died three years ago.

JOYCE   I'm sorry.

GEORGE   She was swimming in the ocean and must have
gone out too far....

Pause.

GEORGE   D'you ever think things might have been
different?

JOYCE   I day dream all the time.

GEORGE   Are you interested in a relationship?

JOYCE   I get restless.

GEORGE   Restless?

JOYCE   I like to forget myself. I love taking chances.
I've made a lot of money that way. I could go
anywhere, do anything.... You shouldn't get
involved with me. I'm not very reliable.

GEORGE   There's a moment, when my consciousness
shifts... I feel my properties melting, everything
I've ever known or felt... nothing holds... it's
terrible... but after a few moments I become
adjusted... I take on that new life. It's been
happening for three years now.

JOYCE   Look that story was funny last night but....

GEORGE   I remember once... I found myself walking down
a residential street late at night. There were no
trees and a huge moon in the sky. All the houses
were made of wood with small windows and
phosphorescent geometric flowers painted on the
shutters. I was lost. I went up to one of the

houses and knocked. A tall, grey being, shaped like a human but with no nose answered. He wore a short tunic with jewelled medallions and said "Come in will ya?" I noticed there was no furniture. The family was all seated on the floor. I stepped in and they clapped — they had hands — and the tall, grey being rippled as he walked, as if he had no bones. The woman of the house looked like a chicken. When I got within three feet of her she turned around and expanded her backside like a huge rose — she was giving off some sort of scent to welcome me. Standing in the shadows I saw a man I thought I knew. He took my arm and led me out to a field where two men were building with a pile of small rocks.

> *A voice shouts "block" from offstage. The lights fade on* JOYCE, *who remains upstage. A man enters carrying a stone block and sets it down near* GEORGE. *As he exits a second man repeats the action. They continue to fetch blocks from offstage throughout the next scene, occasionally calling "slab" or "block." Their appearnace should suggest victims of a failed experiment. A third man, the guide, played by the scientist, enters and stands beside* GEORGE.

GEORGE   Why are they wearing masks?

GUIDE   Their faces are horribly disfigured.

GEORGE   What are they doing?

GUIDE   Building.

GEORGE   Building what?

GUIDE   I'm not sure.

GEORGE   Why don't you ask them?

GUIDE	They wouldn't understand me.
GEORGE	Why not?
GUIDE	Their language only has three words.
GEORGE	I know two of them.
GUIDE	"Slab" and "Block."
GEORGE	What's the third?
GUIDE	"Hilarious."
GEORGE	That's the word?
GUIDE	Yes.
GEORGE	"Hilarious"? What can they do with that?
GUIDE	Nothing.
GEORGE	How can you have a language with only three words?
GUIDE	Some say they were once an advanced civilization. There was a war. Somehow their memories were selectively destroyed. Only three words survived. Others say they're a very primitive civilization. They learned the first two words by trial and error, and somehow stumbled on the third... a tourist perhaps. Others say they're an ordinary civilization but very concise. It would take fifty encyclopædias to translate the meanings of "slab" and "block" into our language.
GEORGE	What d'you say?
GUIDE	Someone tampered with their brains.
GEORGE	Why?

GUIDE	Some biologists believe that mental processes create a field of information.
GEORGE	I don't understand.
GUIDE	I'm going to kill you. In every world.
GEORGE	But I haven't done anything.
GUIDE	You will.

> *Lights rise on* JOYCE. *The* GUIDE *exits.* JOYCE *stretches as if waking.*

JOYCE	What time is it?
GEORGE	Ten.
JOYCE	How long have you been awake?
GEORGE	Not long.
JOYCE	I don't know what you did to me. I haven't slept like that in years.
GEORGE	Must have been the alcohol.
JOYCE	I wasn't *that* drunk.

> *Pause.*

JOYCE	What's that smell?
GEORGE	Coffee. I'm making coffee.
JOYCE	D'you have any plans for today?
GEORGE	No.
JOYCE	No plans. I've been late at the lab three days this week. And when I'm there I can't concentrate. My colleagues think I've cracked.

GEORGE	(*looking at the blocks by his feet*) Why do you have so many stones in your apartment?
JOYCE	My ex-boyfriend left them. He was a sculptor. He brought them from the sea.
GEORGE	You didn't tell me about him.
JOYCE	We broke up a week before I met you.
GEORGE	Were you in love?
JOYCE	We were going to be married.
GEORGE	What happened?
JOYCE	I found out he was seeing someone else at the same time.

Pause.

JOYCE	When I was at the lab he would bring her here. Now he sends me presents every day. I don't know how someone can lead two different lives.

Pause.

GEORGE	I've never been unfaithful.
JOYCE	How many lovers have you had?
GEORGE	(*holding up his hand*) I could count them on the fingers of one hand.
JOYCE	How many times?
GEORGE	I'm serious. I was married before I was twenty.
JOYCE	(*taking his hand, kissing his fingers*) I love the way you touch me.

They kiss.

JOYCE	Are you thinking about her now?
	Pause.
JOYCE	No answer. You're so passive — like smoke — I could put my hand through you. Here — push against me — you see, there's nothing there. Maybe that's why you touch me so lightly.
GEORGE	There's a place I'd like to show you.
JOYCE	Where?
GEORGE	Near the ocean. It's very secluded.
JOYCE	I'm sorry — I really can't afford to take time off now.
GEORGE	I think you'd understand me better if you came with me.
JOYCE	I can't. Things are very competitive at work right now.
GEORGE	You'll think more clearly if you have a rest. It will help us both.
JOYCE	You really are trying to ruin me.
GEORGE	We could have everything.
JOYCE	I don't want everything.
GEORGE	Even for a few days.
JOYCE	Alright.

Scene Ten

> JOCELYN's *voice is heard in the darkness.*

JOCELYN   Imagine a candle. Those of you who scored less than ten on the visualization exercise should use a real candle.

> *A match flares.* WILLIAMS *lights a candle.*

This will only be necessary for the first few days. After that you should be able to see the bright magic of the flame in your mind's eye simply by closing your eyes and fixing your gaze at a spot in the centre of your forehead.... Is your candle lit? Good. Sit three feet away from your real or imaginary candle and relax.

> WILLIAMS *sits.*

The flame is soothing to look at. Focus your attention on it while the specially edited Baroque music plays. (*as music starts*) While your attention is focused, attain what Wordsworth called "a happy stillness of mind."

> BERKLEY *enters.*

Now get ready for a journey to the beach.

BERKLEY   Surf's up.

WILLIAMS   Oh, hello chief.

JOCELYN	See yourself sitting on a beach in Florida.

WILLIAMS *turns off the recorder.*

BERKLEY	What are you doing?
WILLIAMS	Just trying to improve myself.
BERKLEY	(*examining the tape.*) By imagining things?
WILLIAMS	It's a good course. Yesterday I learned that we only use a tenth of our brains.
BERKLEY	In your case I'd say that's true.
WILLIAMS	What's the matter with you? You're very irritable. You're not yourself lately.
BERKLEY	It's not me that's changed. When I was young, police work used to be simple. If something was missing you had a good idea why. Not how. But at least why.
WILLIAMS	You've got plenty of leads.
BERKLEY	We don't even know how they cut the skulls! Two of the apartments were locked from the inside. There's a murderer running around this city who seem to be able to walk through walls.

A MAN enters during BERKLEY 's speech and stands behind him.

MAN	Are you Inspector Berkley?
BERKLEY	(*surprised*) Yes.
MAN	I'm a friend of George Barber. That is... I was a friend.
BERKLEY	A friend?

MAN	Well, not a friend... an acquaintance. We used to talk sometimes in the hall... about my ideas. I'm the caretaker in his building.
BERKLEY	D'you know anything about his death?
MAN	The night he was murdered I was on the roof. I saw a light.
BERKLEY	A light?
MAN	Yes.
BERKLEY	What sort of light?
MAN	In the sky. As it came closer I saw it was five lights in a row — each about ten feet across.

Pause

BERKLEY	Are you saying you saw flying saucers?
MAN	Yes.

Pause.

MAN	If the Nazis had won World War II we'd be ready. Genetic engineering would have given us the advantage. Now they're stealing our brains.
BERKLEY	Thank you for the information. We'll get back to you.
MAN	There's a world-wide battle for the control of our brains!
BERKLEY	We'll look into it.
MAN	Thank you.

MAN *exits.*

BERKLEY	This morning someone phoned and said they're turning the brains into vitamins.

WILLIAMS   Where are you going?

BERKLEY   I've got a few more leads.

WILLIAMS   You want me to come with you7

BERKLEY   No.

WILLIAMS   Be careful. You don't look so well.

> BERKLEY *exits.* WILLIAMS *turns on the recorder.*

JOCELYN   Imagine the waves breaking on the hot sand....

Scene Eleven

>   *Lights up on* GEORGE, *and* JOYCE
>   *who is examining a photograph.*

JOYCE   It's beautiful.

GEORGE   The picture doesn't do it justice.

JOYCE   Why aren't there any people on the beach?

GEORGE   It's not easy to get there. You have to climb out
                     over some rocks.

JOYCE   How did you find it?

GEORGE   My wife used to swim there.

>   *Pause.*

JOYCE   You were talking in your sleep last night.

GEORGE   What did I say?

JOYCE   Slab and block. Over and over. I'd say you
                     should come into the lab. I could run some tests.
                     I could probably write a paper on you.

GEORGE   (*looking at his watch*) Shouldn't you be at work?

JOYCE.   No.

GEORGE   What's happened to you?

JOYCE   I've gotten lazy. You've infected me.

GEORGE	I thought you loved your work.
JOYCE	Yesterday there was a demonstration at the lab.
GEORGE	About what?
JOYCE	One of my colleagues. He's keeping an ape's brain alive. I've never seen a crowd so angry. They believe it's in pain.
GEORGE	You should call the police. Those people are fanatics.
JOYCE	Sometimes I wonder what I'm contributing to.
GEORGE	You have a duty.
JOYCE	To use other life?
GEORGE	To investigate every fact.
JOYCE	More facts, more theories. I work knowing that every idea I have is about to be thought of by someone else. Or already has been. Why should I add one more thought to the pile? There are too many words and most of them outdated. When I was a teenager, I tried to develop a mathematical approach to literature. I invented the meaning decay coefficient.
GEORGE	What's that?
JOYCE	The rate at which a word becomes meaningless over time.
GEORGE	That sounds promising.
JOYCE	I'm not a very good scientist. As a biologist I've seen how everything struggles for more — more food, more protection, more life. But I also know that what you have is always relative to what you can imagine. That's why I try to keep my

mind occupied and focused. If I think too much about how things might have been I just get depressed.

GEORGE   You're too strong.

JOYCE   No. I've changed.

Pause.

JOYCE   This morning when I woke up I couldn't remember where I was. I thought I was someplace new... in another time... not the past or future — a place different from any present place. I haven't felt that kind of exhilaration since I was a child. I'd float down at the bottom of the lake watching the sunlight on the rocks, trying to imagine what it would be like to have gills. I knew one breath would let a whole other world in.

Pause.

JOYCE   I wasn't cut out to be a stock broker.

GEORGE   What? What did you say?

JOYCE   I said I wasn't cut out to be a scientist.

Pause.

JOYCE   What's the matter? Are you alright?

GEORGE   I'm fine.

JOYCE   Let's leave tonight. I could use a rest. (*kissing him*)

Scene Twelve

>WILLIAMS *stands near a body covered by a blood stained sheet.* BERKLEY *enters.*

BERKLEY What have you got for me, Williams?

WILLIAMS Number eleven.

BERKLEY Male or female?

WILLIAMS Male. (*he holds up a brain bag*)

>BERKLEY *lifts the sheet and looks at the corpse.*

WILLIAMS We searched the whole apartment. No trace of anything. The door was locked from the inside.

BERKLEY This morning I got a call from Twelfth Precinct. They found that caretaker we talked to locked in the freezer of the plant where he worked. He had all the symptoms of having frozen to death... but the freezer wasn't turned on.

WILLIAMS What?

BERKLEY He froze to death at room temperature.

WILLIAMS You think there's a connection to this?

BERKLEY Yes.

WILLIAMS What is it?

                Pause.

BERKLEY   I've never felt so helpless in my life.

                Pause.

WILLIAMS   Looks like rain.

                Pause.

WILLIAMS   What are we going to do, chief?

BERKLEY   Nothing. Absolutely nothing.

Scene Thirteen

The sound of heavy rain. Lights up on GEORGE. JOYCE speaks from off stage.

JOYCE   I can't believe this rain. We're going to be washed away. I hope you didn't get too wet.

GEORGE   No.

JOYCE   You must be freezing. I'll put your coat in here so it dries off.

GEORGE   Thanks. (*picking up a bowl and examining it*)

JOYCE *enters.*

JOYCE   Pretty isn't it?

GEORGE   (*still looking at the bowl*) Yes.

JOYCE   You won't believe who I saw at lunch today.

GEORGE   Who?

JOYCE   Susan Kale. (*pause*) You remember Susan?

GEORGE   No.

JOYCE   I sold her a thousand shares of Gentech this morning. You talked to her for over an hour. The woman who... You haven't heard a word I said.

GEORGE   Sure I have.

JOYCE	What are you doing? You've been staring at that bowl for five minutes.
GEORGE	Comparing it.
JOYCE	To what?
GEORGE	Itself.

Pause.

JOYCE	Don't you need something else?
GEORGE	What?
JOYCE	Well, you see, most people... that is, on this planet... when they compare something, they compare it to a second thing. It's a quaint custom we have.
GEORGE	How d'you know it's only one thing?
JOYCE	Because my ex gave it to me.
GEORGE	I don't follow.
JOYCE	He would never give me two things without pointing both of them out very clearly and going on about how much they both cost. Therefore, it's one thing.
GEORGE	But it could have been a lot of things.
JOYCE	Sure, it could have been a beach and we could be sitting on it.
GEORGE	That's what I'm comparing it to.
JOYCE	Right.
GEORGE	I think we should leave tonight.
JOYCE	I don't think so.

GEORGE	Why not? You can afford to take some time off. You're overworked as it is.
JOYCE	It's not work.
GEORGE	What is it?

Pause.

JOYCE	I'm not happy.
GEORGE	What d'you mean... Joyce?
JOYCE	In the beginning, it was all very casual and fun, now all of a sudden you're here every night. It's gotten too claustrophobic.
GEORGE	I can give you more freedom. I won't come over so often.
JOYCE	It's not just that.
GEORGE	What is it?
JOYCE	It's us. When I imagine us together, I like us. We seem perfect for each other. I always think I'm going to enjoy our times together, but as soon as you're here there's always something missing. I've had a lot of fun with you, but sometimes when you smile it's aimed a million miles behind me.... I never know what's going on inside your head. My friends don't know what to make of you.

Pause.

GEORGE	I heard of someone once who lost his arm in an accident. About three years later he began to feel as if his arm was still there. (*reaching for her*) Sometimes he would reach for things and realize he couldn't pick them up. And the arm was always in pain, a kind of buzzing, stinging pain, like bubbles exploding in his hand. He couldn't predict the pain, he couldn't concentrate...

sometimes he couldn't finish a sentence... and he couldn't believe people didn't see how bad the pain was... he expected them to see his hand jumping around and pulsating. (*sitting down and holding his head*) You can't imagine how I feel. For me it's not just an arm... I can't tell you....

JOYCE   Look, you're not making this very easy.... I had a carefully rehearsed speech... but now I can't seem to remember anything. I'm not doing this very well. The point is... I've met someone.

GEORGE   What?

JOYCE   I've been seeing someone for three weeks. I met him at work. He's very different from you. I'm not saying better — but we have a lot of fun together, and he's offered me... more.

GEORGE   More what?

JOYCE   More life.

Pause.

JOYCE   D'you want a lift anywhere? It's pouring rain.

GEORGE   No thank you, I....

JOYCE   I'm sorry it had to be this way.

Pause.

JOYCE   I didn't have to tell you all this. I could have just stopped answering your calls. But I thought it would help if you knew what I felt. Next time... for your next relationship.

GEORGE   This wasn't a rehearsal....

JOYCE   Please, don't.

GEORGE   You were the only one... in every world....

JOYCE   I'm trying to be rational about this.

GEORGE   My love is infinite.

JOYCE   You'll find someone else. There are plenty of....

GEORGE   He's going to kill me.

JOYCE   Who?

GEORGE   Joyce, please....

JOYCE   Look, you're scaring me. If you don't get out, I'll call the police. (*picking up the telephone*) I'm warning you.

GEORGE   No, don't.

JOYCE   Get out!

                    JOYCE *dials.* GEORGE *moves towards her.*

Scene Fourteen

> *The telephone rings.* BERKLEY *sits staring into space. The phone stops.* WILLIAMS *enters.*

WILLIAMS What's the matter, chief? You didn't answer the phone. You've been sitting there for days. You haven't moved from that chair for three days!

BERKLEY (*to himself*) A rat can only imagine so much....

WILLIAMS What? What's that?

BERKLEY Suppose a rat had an enemy....

WILLIAMS What kind of enemy, chief? Another rat?

BERKLEY No. Like us.

WILLIAMS Like us?

BERKLEY (*looking at the brain of the rat*) There's no way the rat could foresee what it's enemy was going to do, because it couldn't even imagine it....

WILLIAMS Unless it was a very smart rat.

BERKLEY No, Williams, it's limited by the structure of its brain. It can't even form the right kind of thoughts.

WILLIAMS Oh.

BERKLEY And we're up against the same kind of enemy.

Pause.

WILLIAMS   So what do we do?

BERKLEY   Nothing. There's nothing we can do. We're fucked.

WILLIAMS   Oh.

BERKLEY   We'll just have to hope that whatever it is leaves us in peace. (*pause*) We're nothing, Williams, in the scheme of things.

WILLIAMS   Oh, I wouldn't go that far....

BERKLEY   This morning I stood in the middle of the street, just stood there and watched the traffic....

WILLIAMS   That's not like you, chief.

BERKLEY   I stood in the middle of the street and people swept by me like I wasn't there. I felt like a ghost. I've got a few more cases to solve and then I'm going to retire and die. What kind of life is that?

WILLIAMS   The pension's not bad.

BERKLEY   I still remember something that scientist said. He said to me — Do you think the numbers didn't exist before we humans found them? Do you think the number two didn't exist? Every thought you can think, officer, existed before you did. And those thoughts affect us. The possibilities swarm around us.... Sometimes you can almost see them. They....

As BERKLEY *speaks,* WILLIAMS *rolls up some paper and circles around the desk. He swats at something.*

WILLIAMS   Aha!

BERKLEY   What are you doing, Williams?

WILLIAMS	This brain seems to be attracting flies. I think it's leaking. It smells awful. (*light flashes*) Look at that... its light went on.

The light blinks on a few more times.

WILLIAMS	What's happening? I think it's trying to signal us.
BERKLEY	Don't be ridiculous. It's hungry. It's trying to get food.
WILLIAMS	How can we help it?
BERKLEY	We can't. (*light flashes*)
WILLIAMS	I can't stand it!
BERKLEY	It's not real, Williams. It's not really hungry.
WILLIAMS	But she thinks she is.

Pause. The light blinks on.

BERKLEY	(*upset*) Look, I've got other cases. I don't have all day to hang around here. I'll see you later.
WILLIAMS	Right, chief.

BERKLEY exits.

WILLIAMS	(*light flashes*) I'm sorry, Louise. (*light flashes*) There's nothing I can do. (*pause*) I don't know how to help you. (*pause*) But there's someone who does. (*picking up the box*)

Scene Fifteen

> *Sound of waves.* JOYCE *sits in a deck chair reading.* GEORGE *enters and sits beside her.*

GEORGE   It's a beautiful view, isn't it?

JOYCE   Yes.

GEORGE   Have you been in swimming?

JOYCE   Yes. The water's lovely. (*going back to her book*)

GEORGE   Are you a good swimmer?

JOYCE   (*a little surprised*) Well, yes... I suppose so....

GEORGE   I love this time of evening. When the water seems to contain every colour.

> JOYCE *goes back to her book.*

GEORGE   How've you been keeping Joyce?

JOYCE   How do you know my name?

> *Pause.*

GEORGE   There was a time... quite a few years ago....

JOYCE   You do look familiar. I've forgotten your name.

GEORGE   George.

JOYCE	George! Yes, of course. George....
GEORGE	Barber.
JOYCE	George Barber! Of course. We were at Cambridge together.
GEORGE	No.
JOYCE	You weren't at Cambridge?
GEORGE	No.
JOYCE	You owned a clothing store on Church Street!
GEORGE	No.
JOYCE	You're keeping me in suspense. How do I know you?
GEORGE	We used to live together. We were married once.

Pause.

JOYCE	I think you're mistaken.
GEORGE	I wouldn't forget a thing like that.

JOYCE *moves to stand up.*

GEORGE	No, please, don't go.... Are you still studying the brain?
JOYCE	Yes.
GEORGE	Dating anyone?
JOYCE	Yes, in fact he's here right....
GEORGE	Found a way to increase intelligence?
JOYCE	How d'you know so much about me? Who set this up? Did Bob....

GEORGE It's not a joke.

JOYCE I don't know you.

GEORGE I've always been interested in the brain. I heard an interesting story once. A neurotic young man asked a psychologist how he could find peace of mind. "How can you lack anything," said the psychologist, pointing to his head, "when you possess the greatest treasure in the universe?"

JOYCE Well, that's a very interesting story, but I'm afraid I have to go.

GEORGE Please don't.

JOYCE I'm afraid you have me mixed up with someone else.

GEORGE Turn around.

JOYCE No.

GEORGE Turn around. (*turning her*)

JOYCE Let go of me!

GEORGE You see, you have a mole on your shoulder. I'm not insane.

JOYCE Let go! Help!

GEORGE *puts his hand over her mouth.*

GEORGE I'm not going to hurt you, Joyce. I love you. I've always loved you.

JOYCE *bites* GEORGE's *hand. He screams and a man calls from offstage.*

VOICE Hey!

GEORGE *runs off.*

Scene Sixteen

GEORGE *is sitting in an office being questioned by a doctor, played by* PENFIELD.

GEORGE I can hardly say I have a memory, Doctor.

DOCTOR Why not?

GEORGE It would be more accurate to say in the collection of people I call me, a memory occurs.

DOCTOR Do you believe in the soul?

GEORGE I used to think there was something extra... something that went along with all the changes, but now I don't think so.

DOCTOR Why did you attack that woman?

Pause.

GEORGE I don't know. I lost control.... I regret it.

DOCTOR What do your other selves think about it?

GEORGE Most of them don't know about it.

DOCTOR Oh?

GEORGE When I believed I had a soul, I was imprisoned in myself. I felt I had to be consistent among my lives. But now I realize they're all different and I can enjoy them all. If there's a unity that makes them all me, I don't know what it is. This is simply a world where I happen to be a criminal. It's not very important. Have you ever imagined killing someone? It's about as important as that. There are so many worlds.

GEORGE *starts to cry.*

GEORGE   Sometimes when I'm falling asleep, I think I'm floating in the sea... two inches below the surface... rocking in the warm salt water like someone who's drowned. Above me the sky is full of clouds, but they're hard-edged like glass. The whole sky glitters like glass. I close my eyes and hear voices, and when I open them again I'm surrounded by a net of branches that grow right into my skin.

Water starts to run down the walls of the room.

DOCTOR   I'm afraid we're going to have to keep you here for a little while, under observation.

GEORGE   That's alright. I have nowhere to go.

DOCTOR   You could go anywhere if you really wanted.

GEORGE   No.

Pause.

GEORGE   I know where I am now. There's only one world. I've been dreaming.

Pause.

GEORGE   I'm in a case.

Scene Seventeen

Sound of the ocean. BERKLEY *works at his desk.* WILLIAMS *enters.*

WILLIAMS   Morning, chief.

BERKLEY   Morning.

WILLIAMS   You have a good weekend?

BERKLEY   Yes. I went away to the beach with my wife. I feel like a new man.

WILLIAMS   You want me to get you some coffee?

BERKLEY   Sure. That would be great.

Pause.

WILLIAMS   By the way... those brains we were looking for....

BERKLEY   Yes.

WILLIAMS   I found them.

Pause.

WILLIAMS   I went to see that scientist, Penfield — took back the rat's brain. He had a bunch of human brains locked up in a cupboard. Hooked up to lights just like that rat. Here's my report.

BERKLEY   (*taking the report*) Thank you.

WILLIAMS   I asked Mrs. Barber, the wife of the... brain that was married to come down. She's here now. You want to talk to her?

BERKLEY   Yes. Thank you.

WILLIAMS *turns to exit.*

BERKLEY   Good work, Williams.

WILLIAMS   Thanks chief.

WILLIAMS *exits.* BERKLEY *reads the report.* WILLIAMS *enters with* JOYCE.

WILLIAMS   In here.

JOYCE   Thank you.

WILLIAMS *exits.*

JOYCE   I understand you found the man who killed my husband.

BERKLEY   Yes.

JOYCE   That's something, I suppose.... But it won't bring him back to life.

BERKLEY   He's still alive.

Pause.

BERKLEY   We found his brain... in a cupboard... hooked up to a life-support system. According to Dr. Penfield, he won't survive more than a few weeks.

Pause.

BERKLEY   He's floating in an aquarium supported by wires. He's downstairs if you'd like to see him.

JOYCE   No thank you.

Pause.

JOYCE   I was just getting adjusted to his death... it's hard... we were married before we were twenty. I was the fifth girl he'd gone out with. We were very happy. He was going to leave his job at the market for me. I was going to give up my research to travel around the world with him. He was the most important thing in the world. He meant everything to me... There's so much we didn't do.

BERKLEY   What would you like me to do with the brain when it stops... functioning?

JOYCE   Donate it to science.

BERKLEY   What?

JOYCE   It was a joke, Inspector.

Pause.

JOYCE   I'll bury it in Novar with the body.

Pause.

JOYCE   Is he in pain?

BERKLEY   Dr. Penfield says he was never able to get more than a rudimentary consciousness going. There's a light that flashes occasionally, but we don't know what it means. Your husband probably isn't aware of who he is. Penfield described it as a kind of fluctuating dream state. Very discontinuous.

Pause.

JOYCE   If I hadn't left him alone that day... it would never have happened.

BERKLEY   You can't blame yourself.

JOYCE   We fought over the stupidest thing. A man at work had given me a present.

Pause.

BERKLEY   If there's anything I can do to help....

JOYCE   No.

Pause.

JOYCE   The hardest thing is knowing he's alone....
D'you think he remembers me? He once said that every second thought was about me.

BERKLEY   I'm sure he's thinking about you somehow....

Scene Eighteen

> *Sound of the ocean, distorted, as if
> contained within a layer of glass. Lights
> up on* JOYCE *and* GEORGE. JOYCE
> *carries a sheet.*

JOYCE   Careful, it's wet here.

GEORGE   I'm alright.

JOYCE   (*holding him*) You're soaking. That was quite a
fall. You could have broken your arm.

GEORGE   I'm fine.

JOYCE   (*touching the ground*) The sand's a bit damp here.
Good thing I brought a sheet.

> JOYCE *spreads the sheet and sits.*
> GEORGE *picks up a rock.*

GEORGE   There must be a thousand fossils in these rocks.
So many failed ideas. (*taking a deep breath*) You
can smell the waste here.

> GEORGE *sits beside* JOYCE.

JOYCE   Tomorrow, if it's nice, we'll go swimming.

GEORGE   Sure.

> GEORGE *kisses* JOYCE.

JOYCE   You're so happy today.

GEORGE	It's nice to be off work.
JOYCE	I'm glad we decided to come here.
GEORGE	I knew you'd like it here — it's one of my favorite spots.

Pause.

JOYCE	It's strange.
GEORGE	What?
JOYCE	Why are we the only ones on the beach?
GEORGE	It's late.

Pause.

JOYCE	It's beautiful here.
GEORGE	It's heaven.
JOYCE	You've been there too?
GEORGE	Oh yes.
JOYCE	What's it like?
GEORGE	Heaven is very strange. I'd go there again, but I'd pack differently.

Pause.

JOYCE	I've always wondered why we have imaginations. One day I'll write a paper. When I was a little girl I used to think it was a different world I saw under the water.
GEORGE	What kind of world?
JOYCE	I really can't put it into words.
GEORGE	Try.

JOYCE	I can't.

Pause.

JOYCE	The word "not" is really magical. I could describe something and say — "But it's *not* that, it's something more" — and you'd know what I meant. It's a way of getting around our ignorance. That's how they used to describe God. Everything we can't conceive of. We say "Things might not have been the way they are," and feel free or uneasy. But there's really nothing behind it. Just a bunch of ghostly possibilities. Because, in the end, everything simply is.

Pause.

JOYCE	How's your arm?
GEORGE	Fine.
JOYCE	(*taking his hand*) You have the most beautiful fingers. They're so soft. (*kissing each of his fingers*) One for each of your lovers. (*pause*) It's almost dark. Soon there'll be stars. We'll have to make a wish.
GEORGE	I thought you didn't wish.
JOYCE	Only for what's possible.
GEORGE	Does that include me?
JOYCE	Yes. I couldn't ask for more.

They kiss.

JOYCE	Look.... What's that light?
GEORGE	Where?
JOYCE	Out there... blinking on and off.
GEORGE	It's a buoy to warn the ships.

JOYCE	There couldn't be shoals that far out.
GEORGE	Why not....
JOYCE	No, look... that flash was longer. (*standing*) Someone's signaling us.
GEORGE	Are you sure?
JOYCE	What should we do?
GEORGE	I don't know. We're miles from a phone.
JOYCE	Someone could be drowning out there.... What should we do?
GEORGE	I don't know!

Pause.

JOYCE	It's stopped.
GEORGE	Thank God..... Whatever it was, there's nothing we can do about it. The coast guard will see it.

Pause.

JOYCE	I'm cold.
GEORGE	Sit down. I'll hold you.
JOYCE	(*sitting beside him*) We should go back soon.
GEORGE	Yes.

Pause.

GEORGE	We'll go away for a year.
JOYCE	A year?
GEORGE	Yes. We'll keep moving. We'll never be alone. We don't want to be sixty, regretting all the things we never did.

Pause.

JOYCE Where will we go?

GEORGE Everywhere.

> *They lie down and hold each other. The lights fade. Far away, in the darkness, a small light blinks on and off several times.*

The End.

Other plays by John Mighton

Body and Soul
Coach House Press
available from Playwrights Union of Canada
ISBN:0-88910-474-3 / $12.95

To what extent is our desire conditioned, and what forms will our desire take when we are given the means to simulate any experience? *Body and Soul* travels to a place where love, biology, and technology meet with surprising results.

"A slightly surreal comedy-drama about necrophilia and virtual sex... full of juicy scenes and lines.
The Globe and Mail

"...thought-provoking, intelligent, insightful, well written...."
CBC Radio, *Later the Same Day*

"A wry, provocative, and entertaining discussion of the relationship between technology and human desires and needs...."
Toronto Sun

The Little Years
Playwrights Canada Press
ISBN: 0-88754-548-3 / $12.95

Nominated for the 1996 Governor General's Literary Award - Drama

A play about the passing of time, our own immortality, and the way in which our lives are extended in the bodies and minds of others.

"The play sneaks up on you, so that by the end you feel the weight of years on characters' lives, and the mystery at the heart of even the most ordinary destinies.... suggests, in so very few strokes, how the past is always with us...."
Carole Corbeil

Other plays by John Mighton

Scientific Americans
Playwrights Canada Press
ISBN:0-88754-488-6 / $12.95

A young physicist moves to an army research facility with his fiance,
to continue his post-doctoral studies. The play traces the breakdown of
their relationship, as he is drawn deeply into military research and she is
forced to confront the dangers of her own work in computer science. By
layering images and ideas from contemporary science, the play extends
the psychological and narrative conventions of realistic theatre.

"...hits home with the accuracy of a guided missile...."

Toronto Star

"...one of the few recent plays to deal intelligently with the great issues
of science in our civilization...."

The Globe and Mail

A Short History of Night
Playwrights Union of Canada
ISBN: 1-55173-511-3 / $9.00

As religious wars and witch hunts rage outside the castle walls, an
unlikely band of alchemists and astrologers vie to unlock the secrets of
the cosmos. Based on the life of Johannes Kepler, the play draws
disturbing parallels between mediaeval and modern thought.

"...confirms Mighton's status as an intellectually absorbing writer...."

Toronto Star